21st Century Citizen

STOP THE WAR

Dona Herweck Rice

Consultant

Jennifer M. Lopez, NBCT, M.S.Ed.
Teacher Specialist—History/Social Studies
Office of Curriculum & Instruction
Norfolk Public Schools

Publishing Credits

Rachelle Cracchiolo, M.S.Ed., *Publisher*
Conni Medina, M.A.Ed., *Editor in Chief*
Emily R. Smith, M.A.Ed., *Content Director*
Véronique Bos, *Creative Director*
Robin Erickson, *Art Director*
Michelle Jovin, M.A., *Associate Editor*
Regina Frank, *Graphic Designer*

Image Credits: front cover, p1 (top right) sadikgulec/iStock; pp.2–3, p.9 (top), pp.10–11 Joseph Sohm/Shutterstock; p.7 (left) Kyodo/Newscom; p.8 Library of Congress [LC-DIG-hec-29676]; p.11 (right) LOC [LC-USZ62-60242]; p.12 LOC [LC-DIG-ds-07107]; p.13 (left) U.S. National Archives; p.13 (right) courtesy Arthur Wiknik, Jr.; p.14 (top) LOC [LC-USZC4-9904]; p.14 (bottom) Collection of the U.S. House of Representatives; p.15 Helioscribe/Shutterstock; pp.16–17 LOC [LC-DIG-highsm-31214]; p.17 (top) Everett Historical/Shutterstock; pp.18–19 Rob Crandall/Shutterstock; p.20 (middle) LOC [LC-USZ62-97864]; p.21 (left) Carl Iwasaki/The LIFE Images Collection/Getty Images; p.27 (left) Education & Exploration 4/Alamy; p.32 (left) Ben Gingell/Shutterstock; all other images from iStock and/or Shutterstock.

TCM | Teacher Created Materials

5301 Oceanus Drive
Huntington Beach, CA 92649-1030
www.tcmpub.com
ISBN 978-0-7439-2315-6
© 2020 Teacher Created Materials, Inc.
Printed by: 926. Printed In: Malaysia. PO#: PO9231

Table of Contents

Small World

The population of the world is nearing eight billion people. They live across nearly forty billion acres of land. Those are huge numbers. In fact, they are much bigger than most people can easily understand. Yet, all those people across all that land still live within a moment of one another. Technology today breaks down all barriers and distance. As massive as the world is, it can also feel small. Person to person, everyone is just a click, search, or social media message away.

Because of this, it is nearly impossible to stay out of touch with events and needs around the world. People are linked through a network of communications systems and news updates. Throughout much of history, people were able to live their lives apart from the rest of the world. That is not the case today. People are connected in ways unheard of in the past. What happens in one place often affects the rest of the planet. No matter where each person lives today, the people of the twenty-first century are truly citizens of the world.

Growing Fast

The population of the world is growing faster and faster. It took until 1804 to reach one billion people. It took 120 years after that to reach two billion. Another 100 years later, it reached seven billion. If the world population keeps growing at the same rate, it should reach eight billion as soon as 2024.

Social Media History

The first social media website launched in 1997. It was called Six Degrees and had around one million members. Seven years later, Facebook® launched. It is now the largest social media platform in the world. Almost 2.4 billion people use the site each month.

What It Means to Be a Citizen

What does it mean to be a citizen of the world? First, it is important to know what it means to be a citizen.

A citizen belongs to a place. This may be a country, state, community, family, or even the world. As part of belonging, citizens enjoy all the **rights** and privileges those places have to offer. Likewise, citizens have **responsibilities** to those places (and to other citizens). Citizens both take and give back. Without this give and take, citizenry would not function for long. Citizens as a group must be active.

To be a citizen is also a legal matter when it comes to governments. A citizen by law belongs to a state, province, or country. That means the government sees that person as a member of a group. A person may live in a place but not be a citizen there. Being a legal citizen is an official title. In most cases, a person cannot just say they are a citizen. There are official steps that have to happen to make it real.

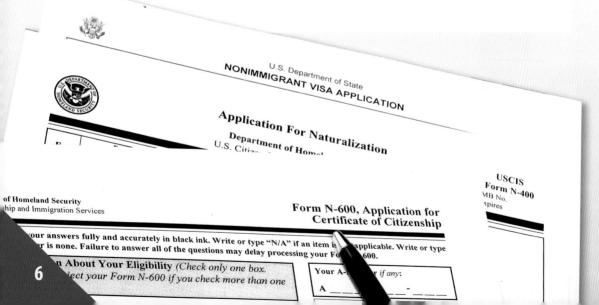

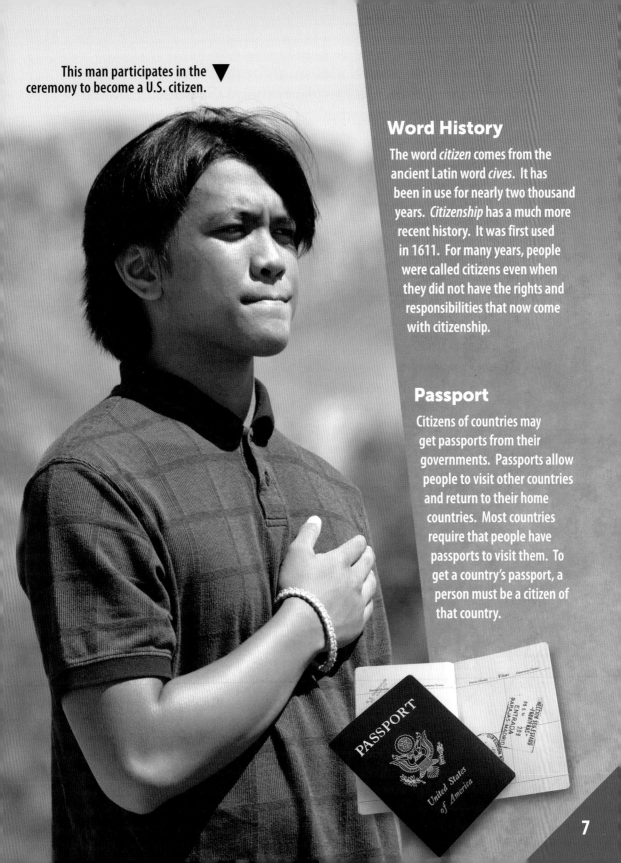

This man participates in the ▼ ceremony to become a U.S. citizen.

Word History

The word *citizen* comes from the ancient Latin word *cives*. It has been in use for nearly two thousand years. *Citizenship* has a much more recent history. It was first used in 1611. For many years, people were called citizens even when they did not have the rights and responsibilities that now come with citizenship.

Passport

Citizens of countries may get passports from their governments. Passports allow people to visit other countries and return to their home countries. Most countries require that people have passports to visit them. To get a country's passport, a person must be a citizen of that country.

Rights and responsibilities are at the heart of being a citizen. These change from place to place around the world. However, the big ideas here are common to most **democracies**.

Rights

All citizens have the same rights. Citizens have the right to be part of their governments. They have the right to participate in them too. Citizens have the right to know what happens in their governments. They have the right to receive protection from their governments. Rights cannot be granted to one citizen but not to all.

▲ This woman fights for her right to vote. The flag's stars show 19 states have ratified the 19th Amendment.

Responsibilities

Citizens have a responsibility to help shape their governments. Voting is a common way to participate. A democracy will fail without people taking part. Citizens also owe their **allegiance** to their countries. A person cannot be a citizen of one place but loyal to another place. Citizens must fulfill any duties they are called upon to perform. (For example, citizens must pay **taxes**.) Citizens must follow all laws. They must also care for the places where they belong.

Voting Laws

Most citizens have the right and responsibility to vote in elections. However, at first, only white males who owned land could vote in the United States. Over the years, though, several **amendments** have been passed and **ratified** to change this. Here are some of the most important voting rights amendments:

15th Amendment (1870)
African American men can legally vote.

19th Amendment (1920)
Women can legally vote.

23rd Amendment (1961)
People in Washington, DC can vote for their representatives.

24th Amendment (1964)
Poll taxes are made illegal.

26th Amendment (1971)
The voting age is lowered from 21 years old to 18 years old.

U.S. Citizen

There are two ways that people can become U.S. citizens at birth. People born in the United States are U.S. citizens. People born in other countries can also sometimes be U.S. citizens. For that to happen, at least one parent must be a U.S. citizen. That parent may be a birth or an **adoptive** parent. They must also live, or have lived for several years, in the United States.

Rights and Responsibilities

U.S. citizens enjoy all the rights the government offers. They can vote in elections if they meet certain requirements. First, they must be at least 18 years old. Second, they must meet their state's requirements for residency. This means they must have lived in an area for a certain amount of time. Usually, the period of time is about one month.

There are some people who are U.S. citizens but who cannot vote. This includes some people who are in prison or who are on **parole**. Part of serving prison time can be losing the right to vote until that **debt** to society is paid. Once that is done, their voting rights may be restored.

Dual Nationality

Some people are dual **nationals**. That means they have rights and responsibilities for two countries. Some governments only allow their citizens to have dual nationality with certain other countries. Some governments do not allow it at all. U.S. citizens are allowed to have dual nationality. Some famous Americans have been dual nationals, including scientist Albert Einstein, who had dual Swiss-U.S. nationality.

Become a Citizen

People who are born in other countries can work to become U.S. citizens. They have to take tests and live in the United States for a number of years. This process is called *naturalization*. Each year, hundreds of thousands of people become naturalized U.S. citizens.

▲ These people celebrate becoming naturalized U.S. citizens.

Citizens may serve in the government. Different positions have different **restrictions**. These are based mainly on age and where people live. For example, to run for state senator, a person must live in that state. To run for president, a person must be at least 35 years old.

Citizens of the United States pay taxes to the government based on their **incomes**. They also pay taxes to their states for property they own. Most states also charge sales tax. That means people who make purchases in those states (even if they don't live there) pay money to the state. All these taxes help support government efforts.

The United States has a system in place to force men into military service if needed. All men between 18 and 25 years old must register for the Selective Service System. This system is used to activate the **draft**. The *draft* is the method by which men are required to serve in the military. The draft can be activated at any time and men who are called must serve. At this time, only men must register; women do not have to. Some other countries have drafts for men and women alike. Some countries require all citizens to serve time in the military. That is not the case in the United States today.

◄ The director of the Selective Service System turns a drum containing draft birth dates in 1972.

Other Rules

People who run for president or vice president must have lived in the country for at least 14 years. They must also be natural-born citizens. That means they were not naturalized. These are the only government roles where people have to be natural-born citizens.

The Draft

The U.S. draft uses a method called "the lottery" to pick the order in which men must report for duty. Under the lottery system, birth dates are randomly assigned numbers. For example, the birth date November 7 might be paired with number 38. That means all men between 18 and 25 who were born on November 7 will be in the thirty-eighth group to report for duty.

▲ This U.S. Marine served in the Vietnam War, which was the last time the draft was activated.

Equal Rights

Citizens of the United States have many freedoms. However, with those freedoms come responsibilities. People may not always see things the same way. However, allowing others to live as they choose is key to being a U.S. citizen. There are laws to protect people's **cultures** and beliefs. This has been true since the Bill of Rights was added to the Constitution. Laws in the United States still support equal rights for all.

U.S. Nationals

Millions of people live in U.S. **territories**. In some of these places, the people are U.S. nationals. In other places, they are U.S. citizens. All people who live in territories have rights. They may live and work in the United States without special permission. Each territory can send one person to the House of Representatives. However, that representative cannot vote. People in territories can't vote in presidential elections either. Some people want to turn these places into states. That would give people there a lot more rights. It would give them more responsibilities too.

◄ Antonio Borja Won Pat was Guam's first representative.

People celebrate at the National Puerto Rican Day Parade. ►

Freedom of Religion

The First Amendment protects freedom of religion. It says that people can practice any religion they want. Or, they can choose not to practice religion at all. The amendment also says that the government can't promote religion. That is why there is no official religion that all people in the United States must practice.

U.S. Territories

U.S. territories have their own governors. Yet, they are still under the authority of the U.S. government. The United States has 5 major territories and 11 smaller ones. All of them are islands or groups of islands. People who live in American Samoa are nationals. People who live in the other territories are citizens. The largest territory is Puerto Rico. It has more than three million people. There are 20 U.S. states that have fewer people than that!

Due Process

One of the key rights held by all U.S. citizens is due process under the law. *Due process* means fair and equal treatment in legal matters. All citizens must be given the same rights when it comes to justice and the law. This is clearly stated in the U.S. Constitution. The Fifth Amendment guarantees it. It says that the U.S. government will not take away people's "life, liberty, or property" without due process of law. This amendment was passed with the Bill of Rights. The founders of the nation saw due process as one of the most important rules of the new country. After the Civil War, another due process amendment passed. The Fourteenth Amendment specifies that state governments also have to follow due process of law.

With due process, every state must honor the rights of its citizens. State governments must treat all people fairly. They must treat people in the same way too. They cannot ignore or change laws for one person or group of citizens. In fact, a person who has been found guilty of a crime may be released if the government does not follow the law. This is how important due process is to all citizens.

▼ The Fourteenth Amendment gave U.S. citizenship to formerly enslaved people.

Article XIV.

Section 1. All persons born or naturalized in the United States, and subject to the jurisdiction thereof, are citizens of the United States and of the State wherein they reside. No State shall make or enforce any law which shall abridge the privileges or immunities of citizens of the United States; nor shall any State deprive any person of life, liberty, or property, without due process of law; nor deny to any person within its jurisdiction the equal protection of the laws.

Due Process History

The Fifth Amendment was meant to keep people's rights safe from the federal government. However, the Civil War proved that state governments could threaten people's rights too. The Fourteenth Amendment was meant to stop that. It also extended the right of due process to naturalized citizens. The Fourteenth Amendment stated that all formerly enslaved people were U.S. citizens. The amendment made it so that all citizens had the right of due process in all situations.

Lady Justice

A famous symbol of justice is a blindfolded woman holding scales and a sword. Lady Justice's scales show that the law must remain balanced and fair. Her sword shows the power of the law. The blindfold stands as a symbol of **impartiality**.

17

Community Citizen

The rights and responsibilities of a U.S. citizen come from both the constitutions of the country and the state. People have the benefit of belonging to both groups. They also have duties to both.

Community citizens have rights and responsibilities too. They are responsible to each other in more personal ways than they may be on the national level. For example, they share the area they live in. They must care for it together. One way they may do this is by keeping their communities clean. Or, they may keep noise low so they don't disturb their neighbors. They may drive safely and respect other drivers and walkers.

Community citizens should also vote in local elections. Local elections decide the leaders and rules that people in communities think are best. It is helpful if everyone speaks up and lets their voices be heard. In this way, rules are decided by most people and not just a few. When people do not vote, they let others make important decisions for them. What matters to them may be ignored.

Making a Difference

The fourth Saturday in October is Make a Difference Day. On this day, people are encouraged to help their communities in some way. Many places host events that people can join. At these events, people can meet and speak with other members of their communities.

Voter Turnout

It is important that people vote for their laws and leaders. That is what it means to be part of a democracy. However, not everyone in the United States votes. The highest voter turnout comes in presidential elections. On average, about 6 out of 10 registered voters show up at the polls. Midterm elections are lower, at about 4 out of 10 voters. Local elections tend to have a very low turnout. In many cities, less than 2 out of 10 people vote in local elections.

Children of a community are citizens too, although they do not have the voting rights that adults have. However, they do have one right and responsibility that adults do not have. Children must attend school.

In the United States, education for children up to a certain age is offered for free. It is not optional. Children do not actually have to attend a public school. But they must be offered schooling equal to what they would receive in public schools. All students must meet the educational standards required by their states no matter where they learn. They must pass the same final tests as well.

◄ school in the 1930s

school today ▶

Brown v. Board of Education

The United States Supreme Court made an important decision in 1954. Schools could no longer be **segregated** by race. Before this decision, separate schools were common. The Brown family of Topeka, Kansas, fought back. They knew the law was not fair. Their fight went all the way to the highest court in the country. The court's decision made school segregation against the law in every state.

Volunteers

Part of what makes some communities strong is having a lot of volunteers. If many people volunteer their time and talents, they can improve communities. They may do this by tutoring young children. Or, they may help at libraries or animal shelters. There are many ways to volunteer!

▲ The Browns and other families protected their children's right to equal education.

Public education was not always mandatory in the United States. As many people's jobs changed from farming to manufacturing, educational needs changed too. People had to be educated for the needs of the jobs. New laws were put in place to require that all children get an education. This also means that all children are *allowed* to go to school. They cannot be put to work instead. And no child can be denied schooling for any reason.

Families

Children may learn a lot about being citizens from their families. It is common for each family member to have rights and responsibilities. They may have chores and other tasks to do in and around their homes. They may have rules about spending time together, such as sharing a meal each day. They may give and receive support from one another in many ways. At their best, each person learns and grows in a family. Each person benefits.

As in communities, family systems function best with give and take. In working together, everyone can succeed. If working against one another, everyone may suffer. When there are problems, working together can create good solutions. When there are needs to be met, working together can create the best results. Maybe the outcome is not what each person wanted most, but it is something that is good for everyone in the end. It is fair and useful. There are no winners or losers but there is a plan that works pretty well for all.

Like with other groups of people, it is all right for people in families to disagree. Everyone does not have to think alike. They just have to come together to **compromise** and create the best outcome for the group as a whole.

Clans

Often in the past—and still in some places around the world—families lived in large clans. Clans may include many mothers, fathers, grandparents, children, and more. Members of clans work together to provide food and shelter for everyone. They help raise children, care for the sick, and help each other in any way needed. Working together makes things better for them all.

There are still clans around the world. In the African Great Lakes region, countries such as Rwanda (roo-AHN-duh) have clans. Some American Indian groups organize into clans. Clans are most common, however, in the Gaelic countries of Ireland and Scotland. Clans there have existed for centuries.

23

World Citizen

To be a citizen anywhere today is really to be a citizen of the world. The world is connected. This is true whether we want it to be or not. There is no place too small or too distant to stay unseen. And so, the rights and responsibilities of citizenship can be said to extend to the whole world.

It may seem as though there is a lot of difference between being a local citizen and being a world citizen. Really, though, they are much the same. Citizens belong to places. They are protected by rights. In turn, they are responsible to their groups. Their responsibilities are meant to benefit them and all others.

The United Nations works to protect the rights of all people. ▼

The rights and responsibilities of world citizenship are like those of other types of citizenship—simply on a larger scale. For example, caring for the environment locally might include picking up trash. Caring for the environment globally might include limiting greenhouse gases. Being a local citizen might mean going out and talking to people in the community. Being a global citizen might mean learning new languages so you can speak to people around the world. All these are important. All of them make a difference in the world.

The Greenhouse Effect

Greenhouse gases have built up over time due to modern engineering. The more fuels people burn, the more gases are released. These gases absorb parts of the sun's radiation. As a result, more and more of the sun's heat stays near Earth instead of escaping back to space.

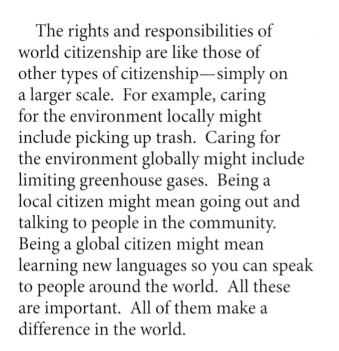

Buying Locally

Global citizens should also pay attention to what they are buying. Whenever possible, buy local goods and food. That cuts down on the transportation it takes to move the items. That means less greenhouse gases will be given off.

Rights and Responsibilities

As a world citizen, each person has human rights. These include the rights to life, freedom, expression, and more. Each person has these rights just because they exist. No matter where a person lives, they should enjoy these rights freely. Through technology, each of us—as citizens of the world—can speak loudly in support of human rights for all people. It is easy today for anyone to see where these rights may be in danger. The citizens of the world can speak together to fight back against injustice and make a change.

We know that the world has become a smaller place. In the past, it was easy to reach out to people in your community. Now, we can connect with people all around the world. In fact, the smaller the world feels, the more important it becomes to support one another. We are entering a time of partnership for people around the world. It is important that we know we are all citizens of Earth. We can depend on one another to succeed. After all, responsibility is at the heart of what it means to be a citizen.

International events can demonstrate how connected the world is. ▶

Doing Your Part

Young people may wonder how they can be actively involved citizens. There are many things they can do. High among them is speaking to family and friends about things that matter. Young people can also help out when they see a need in the world. And as soon as they are able, they can register to vote—and then do it!

Learning More

Global citizenship is important. Many colleges think so too. A lot of schools have classes that teach how to be global citizens. Some schools even offer **degrees** in global citizenship. To earn those degrees, students must show that they understand how the world is connected.

DONATION

-> Connect It! <-

An important part of citizenship is working together for the greater good. Not everyone will do the same jobs, but everyone can be part of making things work for all people. It takes compromise and cooperation. If done well, each person will likely get more than they give.

It is important to understand the rights and responsibilities of other people. That will help you learn more about being a twenty-first century citizen.

1. Find a pen pal who you can write to. (You may want to ask family friends who live far away. Or, you may want to search online to find a pen pal from a school in another country. Be sure to check with an adult before connecting with pen pals online.)

2. Choose a method of correspondence: Will you mail letters or send emails? Will you communicate in another way?

3. Write to your pen pal about a typical day in your life. Include information about what your life is like and what you hope for the future.

Note: Always ask an adult before including personal information in your letters or emails.

Glossary

adoptive—refers to someone who agrees by law to take care of a child or children as their own

allegiance—loyalty to a person, group, country, or idea

amendments—changes to the words or meanings of laws or documents

compromise—to settle differences by having each side give up something they want

cultures—the customs, beliefs, art, and ways of life of groups or societies

debt—a state of owing another

degrees—official documents or titles given to people who have completed classes at universities or colleges

democracies—forms of government in which power is held by the people

draft—a selection of people from the general population for military service

impartiality—treating all people and things equally

incomes—money earned

nationals—people who owe allegiance to or are under the protection of nations and who may or may not be citizens of those nations

parole—a system of early release for prisoners who meet specific requirements

poll taxes—money that people had to pay during voter registration, which made it difficult for all people to exercise their right to vote

ratified—made official by signing it or voting for it

responsibilities—required duties

restrictions—limits

rights—guaranteed freedoms

segregated—separated by race, religion, or other factors

taxes—money paid to a government to support government services

territories—areas of land controlled by governments

Index

Your Turn!

One of the best ways to demonstrate your citizenship is by letting your voice be heard. Think about something that you would like to see changed. It can be an issue at your school, in your community, in your state, or in your country. Learn about why the problem exists. Are there laws in place that are causing the issue? Do people simply not know about the issue? Write to the person with the power to make the change. (It can be your principal, your mayor, your governor, or even your president.) Tell them what the issue is, why it is an issue, and how you think it can be changed.